The
"I'm Not a Salesperson"
Sales Book

Sell Like A Natural Even
If You're Not.

Amy Walker

Dedicated to my 5 sons who are all natural salesmen and talk me into all sorts of things I probably don't need or want, but am usually grateful for in the end. I love you guys. And to my husband Stephen who hates to sell, but takes care of all the details of our lives and business so that I can stay in my lane and do what I'm great at. You are the best family I could ask for.

Foreword:
By Lisa Lieberman-Wang

One day a woman tells me "I hate sales, I always get rejected." I pause for a moment and share that I have been in sales for over 35 years and I have never been rejected. She looks at me startled for a moment and I continue. I tell her they may have rejected my offer, but they didn't reject me. They don't know me well enough to not like me.

You may be offering your prospective client oatmeal raisin cookies and they only like chocolate chip. They are rejecting your product or service not you. The trick is to find out what they want and to give it to them.

If you ever felt like that woman, you're not alone. I learned a long time ago in my sales career from one of my mentors Tom Hopkins that it took 29 "No's" to get 1 "Yes". I would start my day with a sheet of paper with 30 lines on it and every time someone said "No", I would say "Thank You" because I knew I was that much closer to my next "Yes".

My grandfather said when I was born, they slapped me on my butt and said salesperson! I may not be the norm, but I love sales! It is the only profession that if you are working for someone you can make more than your boss. If you are working for yourself, you get to control your income. Sales is the lifeblood of all organizations. Sales is the gift you give others when you fill the gap and help them get what they want and need. Sales is a service of helping others. It is the best career in the world.

It's time to move past the negative connotations you might have with sales, and really embrace the opportunity you have before you.

In my career I have done more than $60 million in sales and have trained over 120k entrepreneurs in sales and marketing. I wish I had this book to share back then as it would have saved so many people years of frustration and learning curves.

Amy Walker paves a path that makes it easy for you to run on. She has taken her 20 years of sales and training experience and put it together in a way to give you a road map to avoid all the pitfalls and to soar to new heights.

Too often you hear people profess to have the answers only to learn that they are talking in theory not proof. They have never walked the walk and are only talking the talk. Amy is not that person. She is a prime example of walking the walk and talking the talk.

She carefully and thoughtfully shows you how to be an amazing salesperson even if you weren't born into it. In The "I'm Not a Salesperson" Sales Book, Amy covers some of the most important aspects of sales that isn't seen everywhere, and she does is masterfully. Her personal journey paved the way for her to bring you the tools and resources to help you whether or not sales is naturally your thing, you will learn to love it.

So often people miss the opportunities because they are using the wrong tool for the job. In this book you will learn how to reset your Sales Mindset, Skillset and take Action as she sets you up for success. You'll learn how to avoid wasting time trying to sell to the wrong people. How to read and deal with different types of people to help them come to a decision. She even gives you templates and formulas to overcome objections and create high conversions into your product or service.

So, your next step is to find a comfortable place to settle in and learn from this brilliant woman, Amy, as she takes you through your own journey to become the greatest salesperson.

Lisa Lieberman-Wang
Success Strategist
www.LisaLiebermanWang.com
#1 International Bestselling Author F.I.N.E. to FAB, TEDx
www.finetofab.com
Co-Founder NAP Coaching Academy
www.NAPCoachingAcademy.com

Contents

INTRO:

My first attempt at sales

What in the world was I thinking?

Two months earlier, I was simply supporting my friend in her new business. Sure I thought she was crazy for selling makeup. Yes, I judged her just a little bit for doing direct sales. But I am a good friend. And that is what good friends do.

Somewhere along the way, I must have lost my mind! Because here I was, a brand new beauty consultant and business owner. And when my sales director promised to help me find clients, this was not what I had in mind.

My husband and I were poor newlyweds. He was still finishing school, I was a new college graduate with a brand new baby. All of our friends were poor. And neither of our families lived in the area. So I really didn't know a lot of people, other than the more established women I went to church with. But they seemed so much older and, to be honest, I was scared to talk to them.

So I told my upline I didn't know anyone to sell to. "That's okay, we'll teach you." She had said it with a bright, encouraging smile, shimmering with a mixture of lipgloss and hope.

Well if this was her idea of teaching, I was in big trouble.

My friend and recruiter had brought me to the mall. "You go this way, I'll go that way." Her air had changed from shimmery hope into something similar to how I imagine soldiers feel right before battle. It was strategic. It was a need to conquer. It was terrifying. "Meet me here in an hour and we'll both have 5 names."

What was I thinking?

I wandered the mall looking like a lunatic for the next hour.

"I like your bag?" I said to a total stranger with a smile of desperation.

"Those are cute shoes. Where did you get them?" I said to another passerby.

"What a cute baby. I have one at home as well." No matter what I said, I just couldn't seem to hook one. They kept sliding right by after a moment of pleasant exchange. (Well, I hope it was pleasant for them. Nothing about this was pleasant for me.)

The timer had 15 minutes left. I couldn't go back empty-handed. I was an intelligent confident woman. I refused to be beat by lipstick!

So I found a woman that was sitting in a cozy armchair reading a newspaper. And I thought, "This is my chance. She can't walk away."

I walked over, stood in front of her and said, "Um, excuse me. I just noticed that you're really pretty ..."

She looked up at me with fear in her eyes. She clearly thought I was hitting on her. And she clearly didn't appreciate it.

"Oh, not like that." I stammered. "It's just, you're really pretty, and I sell make up. And I was wondering if I could ..."

She cut me off. "Yeah, no."

She looked at me like I was insane. I felt insane. I turned around, determined to keep my head held high because I hoped it would hide my dejection.

"Sales is just not my thing," I consoled myself as I walked away. I resolved that I would have to find another way to be successful in business. A way without ever having to talk to anyone again. That was, after all, a terrible experience!

I'm happy to share with you, I've since closed millions of dollars of sales. And to my readers, let me give you a bit of hope. If I can start out that bad and master selling, you can too. And I promise I will never drop you off in a mall and ask you to go stalk strangers!

My deepest condolences to the lady I hit on, all of the women I stalked in malls, Walmart and Target between the years of 2002-2006, and every poor woman I told to do the same thing. I didn't know any better.

Now I do. And you will too.

CHAPTER 1:

How to Sell when Selling Just Isn't Your Thing

I am not a natural-born salesperson. You are not a natural-born salesperson, either. In fact I don't believe anyone is.

Sales, done correctly, is a skill. It's the art of reading people, listening intently, and guiding the client towards a decision. I've yet to meet someone who possessed all of those skills right out of the womb.

And yet, I commonly hear this phrase, "I'm just not a salesperson." And it is somehow supposed to excuse you from learning the art of closing a sale. Sorry, but I'm not buying that story. And I highly recommend that you stop buying it as well. That is an expensive story!

If you are a business owner, you are in sales. If you are an entrepreneur, you are in sales. If you are a network marketer, you are in sales. And if you are looking for a great career where you can always earn high incomes while having a good amount of flexibility, you should consider sales.

As you read this book, you will learn how to sell well. Being great at sales doesn't just mean you close a lot of deals. There are many ways to close more deals. You could ask a million people to buy from you and you would close more deals. You could pressure people into buying from you. You could manipulate them into buying out of fear. You could have a total disregard for the people you sell to and sell them things they don't need, want or benefit from. None of those scenarios make you a great salesperson.

When you are great at sales you are good at connecting with people. You build and maintain trust over long periods of time. You maintain your clientbase and have high retention rates. You have a high closing ratio and consistently move people through your sales system. And the best indicator of being great at sales is that both you and your potential client ENJOY the process.

Did your brain just do a double take? Is it possible to enjoy selling? Is it possible for your client to enjoy being sold to? Absolutely! In fact, sales should always be enjoyable for both parties. If it's not, you're not doing it right!

I know this from first-hand experience. With my first experience with sales, I didn't even realize I was in sales. I was 19 years old, a sophomore in college, and I was recruiting volunteers to go teach English in Russia and China. I had spend a semester abroad teaching and had a truly life-changing experience. I was on a mission to change the world, one child at a time. I felt like everyone should have the same experience I had and so I talked to everyone! There was no awkwardness. Some said yes. Some said no. I knew people all over campus because I had met them discussing teaching abroad. And I had one of the highest success rates of anyone the company had ever hired before. I was so successful that they actually moved away from commission and into hourly rates after my first year. It was a great job for a college student.

My next experience with sales was all kinds of wrong! I had just graduated from college. My husband and I had our first baby and decided I was going to be a stay-at-home mom. That lasted for a good 5 months before I decided to start a direct sales business. I knew I wanted to be home to raise my kids. But I also knew I would go crazy without something to challenge me. So I started a business -- enter the shimmery lipgloss. The problem was, this time, I knew I was in sales. I did everything wrong. I felt like a stalker. I was great at presenting my product. But I got nervous and sweaty when it was time to close deals.

I would fluctuate. I would pretend like I didn't even care if they bought products. I was just there to educate. After all, the products were so good they sell themselves! (Insert all the eye rolls and sarcasm you can get. This is a horrible sales approach and I'll explain why in a later chapter!) And when I was desperate for sales I would come across as needy and, you guessed it, desperate. I was bad. So bad that it took me two to three times as much work as the average sales consultant to get mediocre results. I had very little repeat business. I had to bribe clients to give me referrals. And if it wasn't for the team building side of my business, I would never have made money.

Even though my early years in direct sales were messy, I'm grateful for them. It was those years that taught me how NOT to sell. And it was during that time that I finally got past my fear of selling enough to start analyzing what great salespeople were doing.

Since those days, I have led sales teams to create millions of dollars in new revenue. I've personally closed over 200K in a weekend. I've closed more sales in an hour than we made in a year when I began my sales journey.

There are many great things that happen when you master the art of sales. My favorites are: First, that you gain a sense of control over your life and your finances. There is no catastrophe that I haven't been able to sell my way out of. The months where you have massive unexpected expenses, rather than being crippled with fear and scarcity, you can simply get to work. And second, I love that sales has taught me to truly understand people. Sales done right is a psychological awareness and understanding of another person. These skills make me a better member of my community, a better mother, and a better wife. Life is more fun when you understand how to get people to move and create wins for people.

There are two ways to read this book. Either one is fine with me.

For the cover to cover readers who want to know the ins and outs of becoming a better salesperson: Be forewarned, you'll need to practice skills before you master them. Everything makes sense in theory. But you won't truly grasp the concepts until you implement them in your business. If you are studying this book with your sales team, I recommend that you go at the pace of a chapter a week. The chapters aren't long. But you'll find the greatest improvement if you read the chapter, practice the skill, and then read the chapter again. This approach will give you total mastery of all the skills covered in this book.

The second type of reader is looking for solutions to current sales problems, and needs to see quick improvements. You will utilize the book more like a reference book. Every chapter in the book is written in a way that it can stand alone. If you implement change in any area of your sales, you will create improvement. This is why sales training is so popular. It doesn't take much effort and training to make a difference in your current numbers. I still encourage you to read all of the chapters in the book. But if you have known challenges that you need support in right now, feel free to address those in order of importance.

Either way, you're about to get a great sales education. And the best part is, you'll love the experience of selling to your clients. And they will love the experience of buying from you.

Notes

CHAPTER 2:

The Success Zone: Mindset, Skillset, and Action

C onsider mindset, skillset and action to be the three amigos of your sales success. They are all required. Leave one out, and you'll experience problems with your results.

Mindset

Mindset is critical in sales. The way you feel about money, yourself, your product, and the experience of selling shows up in your sales conversations. If you are asking a customer to spend more on a product than you could personally afford, trust me, it's going to throw your brain for a loop. You'll experience doubt, guilt, and discomfort during the conversation if you don't go in mentally prepared. Unfortunately for all of us, we don't magically become a better version of ourselves when we enter a sales conversation. We bring our fears, doubts, and weaknesses with us. This is why we must actively work on programing our minds for success in order to win in sales.

Here are some strategies that I use in order to get my mind in the right place.

1. Abundance thinking

Scarcity thinking is when your mind predominantly focuses on what is lacking around you. There is not enough time. There is not enough money. You can't afford things. You are always waiting to run out.

Abundance thinking is the opposite. It is when your mind predominantly focuses on how much you have around you. Your brain searches for resources you need in order to create the results you desire. You feel and believe that good things are coming your way. Even when the bank account is sparse, you have confidence that you can replenish the account.

Abundance and scarcity thinking have nothing to do with your reality. They are all about perception. I remember the first time I earned $14,000 in a month I was shocked at how much scarcity thinking I battled. I was worried that it was not going to be enough. I felt like it was just going to come in and go right back out. I felt like no matter how hard I worked it would never be enough. What came up for me were all of the scarcity beliefs I had harbored for years when we were struggling to pay our bills. The increase in money triggered all of my old money beliefs and it kind of freaked out my brain. My reality was not my thinking. But my thinking became my reality. At the end of the month I had indeed spent all of that money and still didn't feel like it was enough. Fortunately, it was a one month relapse into scarcity thinking. I pulled myself out and moved on to have a more healthy relationship with the money I was earning. Perception often creates our reality. That is why you will need to shift yours in order to succeed in sales.

In order to shift into abundance thinking, I recommend reading these companion books by Leslie Householder: The Jackrabbit Factor and The Portal to Genius. These books represented a critical shift for me in my abundance mindset.

2. Connect with money

We all have money beliefs. Most of us inherited them from our parents before we were even old enough to understand what these beliefs meant. My false understanding was that money was the bad guy. Clients would buy from me, if only they had the money. I couldn't go on vacation because I didn't have enough money. I'd have more time with my family, if only I didn't have to go out and earn money.

In order to start closing more deals, I needed money to be on my team. I couldn't despise money and then expect it to show up for me. So I started doing something crazy. On my way to every sales appointment, I would take out a $100 bill and hold it up against my steering wheel while I drove. And I would talk to money.

"Ben (aka Benjamin Franklin), we've got an appointment today. And it's our job to help the people. We are a team, you and I, so let's both do our part. My job is to present the information and ask the questions. Your job is to be with the people and give them permission to move forward with us. I know we can do great things together. Thanks for spending the day with me."

If you are thinking, "That is just too weird. I would never do that," let me assure you that I was never sent to a mental hospital. And I quadrupled my sales. I'd rather be the type of crazy that is happy and making money than the type of sane that is broke and stuck!

3. Be kind to yourself

It sounds so simple, but I can't tell you how many people try to increase their sales by bullying themselves. It's the army drill sergeant approach. First, you constantly berate yourself for all of your shortcomings. Then, instead of finding yourself feeling empowered to make your sales calls, you find yourself with the perfect excuse not to get on the phones. You've got to answer emails, or file those papers, or vacuum. After all, who can successfully close sales with an unvacuumed rug?

I invite you to try a new approach. This time, try encouraging yourself. Celebrate every phone call you make, even if it doesn't feel like enough. Tell yourself how great you will be instead of how much you stink. Be your own best friend and encourage your way into growth.

4. Power phrases

I recommend starting off every day with your mind in a powerful place. I use power phrases to direct my mind where I want it to be. I use them in many areas of my life, but I always have one directed towards my sales.

My first sales power phrase was, "I have a strong relationship with money and time. The Lord blesses me freely with both because I use them to bless others."

Another one I've used is, "Money is my partner and together we create massive amounts of good in the world."

My current money power phrase is, "Money is constantly moving towards me. I treat money with respect. Money loves to partner with me."

I also use my power phrase during the day. Whenever you start to feel a dip in your energy or mindset, reset your thinking by using your power phrase. For me it acts like an anchor. I can't get too far out into the sea of scarcity if I have an anchor keeping me tied to abundance thinking.

Skill Set

It is interesting to me how many people worry about the skill set part of sales, because it is actually the easiest part to master.

We buy into the story that sales just doesn't come naturally to us and therefore we can't really sell with any level of proficiency. In reality, almost anyone can learn to sell. If you truly dislike being around people, sales might not be for you. But if you like talking with people, and are willing to learn how to do that better, then you can learn to sell.

This book is the first step in learning the skills you need. The skills are the easy part!

Activity

Activity is simply going out and doing the work. It's making the calls. Holding the appointments. Overcoming the objections. And closing the deals. It's monotonous in the sense that you do the same thing over and over again. And it's exciting in the sense that you get to talk with new people every day! For me, sales doesn't get boring because I love talking to new people. I love helping business owners solve their problems.

If you are struggling to get to work, let me give you a few words of advice. Fear is an emotion that is supposed to cause movement. Fear sends our brain into fight or flight mode in order to protect us. Fear over sales really doesn't make a lot of sense. Nothing bad is going to happen to us if we do our sales calls. In fact, it's probably going to cause good things to happen. But your brain still sends the trigger. When you start to feel fear come up, the best thing you can do is something. The longer you wait, the more the fear grows. And if you don't create movement, it can turn into paralyzing fear that will become harder and harder with each time you don't start working. There is no possible positive outcome that comes when you do nothing.

On the flip side, if you will pick up the phone or drive to a potential client, the movement will actually shift the fear into manifesting more like excitement. Because now you have positioned yourself in a place where there is a possible positive outcome.

Here's a tip for getting started.

1. Reward yourself. The first 10 attempts are always the hardest to make. So give yourself a reward when you get 10 calls done in an hour, or send out 10 prospecting emails, or do 10 of whatever you do to close deals.. When I was building my discipline I was working entirely on the phone. Texting didn't exist yet. After my first 10 phone calls, I got a drink of water. After the second 10, I got some M&M's. After the third 10, I got to listen to some music. After the fourth 10, I got to take a walk outside. And when I hit 50 calls, I got to go read for an hour. Those little rewards really made a difference.

2. Find an accountability partner. Find another entrepreneur, salesperson, or business owner and challenge each other. Whoever makes the most attempts gets lunch, compliments of the loser. Or base it on results. Whoever gets the most set appointments gets ice cream, compliments of the loser. You choose the rewards and the challenge, and the synergy of knowing you are not in it alone will do wonders for your business.

3. Less thinking, more action. I remember when I was new in sales. I would think of someone I should reach out to. I would tell myself that I would call the lead that evening when she would be home from the office. I would then spend the entire day anticipating the call in my mind. By the time I was ready to actually make the call, I'd already been through it HUNDREDS of times in my mind. I was tired from the mental work and I hadn't actually picked up the phone! Let me be VERY clear. YOU DO NOT GET PAID TO THINK ABOUT WORKING.

I know someone out there is thinking, "But I have to prepare for my sales conversations. I don't want to be caught unprepared." If you have a basic reach out script, you are prepared. If you don't have one, it's time to get one!

That is all the preparation you need. Beyond that, there is no way to anticipate the response you will receive, the questions the person will ask, or how the call will go. There are points in the sales process that require more preparation, but the reach out conversation just isn't one of them.

Mindset, Skillset, and Activity working together

Sales results are at their best when mindset, skillset and activity are ALL in play. A combination of any two of these elements, without the third, will fall flat.

Skillset + Activity

When a salesperson has the skillset and the activity, but doesn't work on their mindset, they experience a difficult journey. They work harder than others to get the same results. It doesn't flow easily to them, and every time they stop to take a break, they feel like they start to lose ground. It's a tiring journey and this brand of salesperson is prone to experiencing burnout.

Activity + Mindset

This combination actually produces more results than the other two combinations. We've all seen it with a new salesperson. They don't know what in the world they are doing, but they're really excited about it. As a result they outsell the experienced sales people. The problem with this is, it's not sustainable long-term. At some point that excitement wears off. And the salesperson, no matter how positive they are, starts to feel the sting of lacking in their skillset. You can't run on enthusiasm forever, but you would be surprised how far it can take you!

Skillset + Mindset

This is my least favorite combination because virtually nothing happens. I've seen far too many people know what to do, spend lots of time focusing on their personal development, and still not get out there and sell. There is no growth because there was never any possibility for growth.

Mindset + Skillset + Activity = Optimal Results!

If you want to truly increase your sales, you're going to have to get to work! Focus a few minutes each morning and night on getting your mind in the right place for success. Read and study the chapters in this book to increase your skills. And then get out there and set appointments! Talk with potential clients. All the training in the world won't increase your sales without some real conversations happening.

Notes

CHAPTER 3:
Qualifying Your Leads

Very few things are a bigger waste of time than having sales conversations with someone who is never going to be able to buy from you. Maybe the service isn't relevant to them. Maybe they are broke and about to be evicted. Maybe they are under contract with another service provider for the next year and cannot switch to your company even if they want to.

Spending time trying to sell to unqualified leads is exhausting, frustrating, and disheartening. It will throw off your sales numbers. If you are working for a company that requires you to close a certain percentage of the people you talk to, this can dramatically lower your closing ratio. If you are a business owner who watches closing ratios, you can't tell if they've dipped because your team is underperforming, or because your lead source stinks.

Stop trying to sell to everyone

You may have a product that works for everyone. It doesn't mean you should sell to everyone. Just because they could use it, does not mean they would enjoy using it, can afford using it, or are that they won't be a pain-in-the-butt client.

The first step is to determine who you want to sell to. Who is your ideal client?

A phenomenal marketer, Michelle Smith, taught me this principle and while I always give her credit, I frequently use it with my clients.

Imagine you were going hunting for elk. You have your equipment and gear. You know how to process the meat. You know what recipes you will use to cook the meat. You want elk. You are ready for elk.

What if a deer crosses your path? Will you take the deer? Will the equipment and gear you brought still allow you to hunt that deer with ease? Will the process of harvesting the meat be similar enough to the elk that your skills will still apply? Can you use the same recipes? In this case, the answer is yes. You may have gone hunting for an elk. But you'll be very happy coming home with a deer.

Now imagine that you are out on your hunt and a porcupine crosses your path. A porcupine has meat on it. You could kill the porcupine and eat it. But think about how much you will have to adjust. Your equipment is all wrong. The harvesting process is different. Who knows what you would even make with porcupine meat? And when it is all said and done, it would be a really big hassle for what you get out of it. You will end up regretting the decision to go after the porcupine. It will feel like a big waste of time and effort for so little return.

We need to be aware of this principle in our businesses.

Case Study:

Kat is an instructional designer and online course builder. She specializes in helping people build better courses, get the course done, and position it so it makes money. She was selling well, but knew she had so much more potential. She wanted to help people launch incredibly successful digital courses. But she was attracting a lot of people who had been in the corporate world for years and wanted to start a business. The problem was, her done-for-you services and high level masterminds were not cheap. So getting people to invest at a high level on something they hadn't really started yet was tricky.

As we talked I realized that her pre-launch clients were porcupines. They took a lot of massaging to get them to buy. And then when they did become clients, they didn't progress well in her sales funnel. They kind of got stuck at the first product.

The elk were established speakers, coaches, and authors who had been in the game long enough to have consistent revenue. This is their main gig. Not a side hustle. And they knew that every new course they develop can be resold for hundreds of thousands of dollars.

Her deer were clients that were even farther along in their careers. They just wanted to skip into the higher level of the funnel. They didn't want to do the events, or the DIY courses. They simply know they need someone to design their courses and manage the project. Because her business already did that type of work, she is prepared for this client, even though they move differently.

3 reasons we try to sell to the wrong clients

While I've seen many reasons why salespeople go after porcupines, they usually fall into these 3 categories:

1. Save the World-

Entrepreneurship is on the rise. And as I write this book, the fastest growing population of new business owners are women. We are flocking to business. And when we step into business, we bring so much more than our awesome shoes, and great networking skills. We bring our compassion. That's not to say that men are not compassionate in their businesses. I've seen both genders use their businesses as platforms for positive social change, and men are not exempt from this problem. However, I see it more frequently in my female clients. We want to help everyone! We want to serve our communities. We want to lift up our neighbors. And if we look more deeply, we don't want to leave ourselves behind.

I remember when I had hit the point in my business that I needed to raise prices. I struggled because I knew that I would not have been able to afford working with me. When I was starting out as an entrepreneur, we were broke. I was a mom, trying to figure out how to balance work and family. I needed skills, but I also needed diapers. And money was tight. When I raised my prices, I knew I was cutting out me and others like me. It was a hard transition.

Let me be very clear with this. The BEST clients are not the ones that are desperate for us to save them. I would not have been a great client for myself. At that time when I needed help, I was also far too chaotic, undisciplined, and afraid to really go out and build a company.

So how do we create a balance between our desire to serve and our desire to sell? It's really quite simple. We do both. I spend time each month using my skill set to serve. And I spend time every month using my skill set to sell to new clients. When I am serving, I don't sell. I'm not looking for clients. I'm simply looking to give back. Because I go in clearly knowing that I'm not going to further my business through this service, I also don't let the service schedule overwhelm my life. I accept one invitation for service a month. Maybe it's speaking to a high school, or a women's ministry, or just a group of emerging entrepreneurs that are not really ready for my help yet. That is what I can manage and still maintain my relationships and growing business.

2. Charlie Brown-

This teaching gem comes from Myron Golden. I attended Myron's One Year Millionaire event in 2014 and absolutely loved this principle. In the Peanuts world, there is a clear social hierarchy. You have the Lucys and Schroeders at the top. However, Lucy and Schroeder are sometimes intimidating. After all, they seem to have it all together. They're probably too busy anyway. And if they said no, well that would be really embarrassing. They would probably tell Violet about it. And once that got out everyone would know. So instead, we approach Sally about our product or service. Sweet, loyal, lovable Sally, who will definitely say yes. She is after all a close relation. And while Sally isn't a bad customer, she's probably not a great one. The trouble starts when referrals start moving through. Sally refers Lynus. Lynus refers Peppermint Patty, Peppermint Patty naturally refers Pig Pen. And all of the sudden, you have a client base of Pig Pens. Maybe your clients are all broke. Or maybe they are all high maintenance. Or maybe they are all single product users, when you are looking for people to adopt your entire line.

Here's where you went wrong. You settled. You knew who your ideal client was, but it was going to take more work to acquire those clients. And it was outside your comfort zone. So instead of putting in the effort to build the connections with where you wanted to go, you settled for available and comfortable. When you know who your ideal client is, hold to that standard. Don't take whatever money comes your way. Find the right money and the right clients for you and your company.

3. One size fits all-

I really dislike seeing one-size-fits-all in clothing stores. I also really dislike seeing one-size-fits-all sales strategies. Most products or services do not serve everyone. If you are truly excited about your product or service, you'll find a need in everyone's life. But, the time you spend convincing the disinterested is wasted time. Even if you have a product that can be used by the old, young, rich, poor, white, black, Muslim, and Christian worlds, it still doesn't mean that you should be selling to all of them.

We need to be honest with ourselves. There are some groups of people that we just don't connect well with. We don't work well with. And it causes us more pain and work than it is worth. I can bring value to almost any type of business. But I am clear that I do not serve all business owners. I know that I don't work well with first time, newbie entrepreneurs, or hobby entrepreneurs. I'm overwhelming to them. They are too timid for me. It's not a match made in heaven. So even though I COULD produce programs for them, and I have in the past. I choose not to. It's not my sweet spot. It doesn't really matter what product you sell, get clear on who you serve the best. Who do you create magic with? And how can you find more of those people?

What is a qualified lead?

Part of working with only the right clients is saying no to the wrong ones. And saying no early on in the process.

Every salesperson should have a written list of defining qualities for a qualified lead.

Here's my list for my Coaching Business. (I have a different list for my speaking business.) The lead must:

- At least 1 year into their business

- Work full time in the business

- Be committed to building structure in the business

- Have a team or be ready/willing to hire contractors

- Have products or services that are currently selling (revenue is moving into the business)

BE READY TO INVEST IN GROWTH: That means time and money

One of my challenges my first year in Direct Sales was that I had no qualifications in place. Basically if it was a woman who was willing to talk to me, I thought I had a great prospect. After the first year of working hard and not making any progress, I upped my qualifications to include someone who was interested in skincare and cosmetics. The year after that I added, "And has money to buy them." I'm sure you can imagine how much harder it was to find great repeat clients in the beginning. I was filling my schedule with porcupines and as a result had very few deer and elk.

Take a moment right now to make your list of qualifications for your ideal clients. Be specific, and write your list down. What exactly do your deer and elk look like? We'll circle back this list later.

2 Step and 1 Step Close

Next we must understand how and when to disqualify a lead that doesn't match your qualifications. I'll teach you two strategies.

Two-Step Close: A two-step close is one where you have two conversations before closing a deal. The first conversation is called the Set. In this conversation, the primary objective is to prequalify the lead, build interest in having a further conversation, and to set an appointment for the actual sales call.

The two-step close process works well because it allows a high volume salesperson to have short conversations with many leads. The appointment setter will cover a lot of ground with the leads. The closer on the team spends more quality time with a lower volume of people. They only spend time with people who are predetermined to be a good fit for the company.

One-Step Close: In a one-step close, you have one salesperson working the leads from start to finish. The goal with this script is to have your qualifying questions positioned at the beginning of the sales call. You would know within the first 10-15 minutes if the lead is qualified. If they are, you go straight into the rest of the conversation. If they are not, you stop the call and let them know that you are not the right person to assist them right now. You can either direct them to a free resource, or refer them to someone you know that would be a better fit for them.

One of the most common reasons I hear people say they don't stop the sales call even when they know the lead isn't qualified is because they feel bad. They desire to help this prospect. So they keep going, hoping they will somehow find a way to make a square peg fit in that round hole.

Here's what happens: The prospect gets their hopes up, and in the end, they still can't afford you, or you still don't have the product they need. It's discouraging for the prospect.

However, if you spend 15 minutes with them, get clear on their needs and their budget and refer them to someone or something that helps them solve their problem, they are usually grateful. I've found they also appreciate the honesty and you not trying to oversell them. They are more likely to refer you to someone that is a fit for you. And they are more likely to circle back around at a later point in time.

If you are unsure of what to say, hang tight, we are moving into sales scripting next!

Notes

CHAPTER 4:
Scripting for Success

I am a big believer in sales scripts. I'm not talking about the kind of script a telemarketer uses on the phone, when you can tell they are reading word for word. They don't even listen to or acknowledge your responses. They just plow onward like a bulldozer that will knock over everything in its way! It's impersonal, unprofessional and to be totally honest, a MAJOR turnoff!

There is a psychological process the brain goes through in order to make a big decision. And your sales script should be helping you to work with the psychology of the mind, instead of fighting against it.

A good sales script should accomplish the following:

1. Give the salesperson confidence. If you have a great sales script, you will walk into each sales conversation feeling confident that

you know what to say, and that there is a high probability that you will close the sale.

2. Make the prospect feel more comfortable. That's right, I said it! One of the reasons I hear people resist sales scripts is that they want their conversations to feel natural and for their prospects to feel comfortable. But guess what is uncomfortable? Being in a conversation where you strongly suspect that someone is trying to sell to you, but you have no idea when the pitch is coming. Your guard is up the entire time. A great sales script will let the prospect know from the very beginning what is going to happen in the conversation and what to expect. It sets the prospect's mind at ease and helps them to be more present in the conversation.

3. Build trust and rapport. A great script will allow you to earn the prospect's trust and allows you to share your knowledge and expertise. Too often I see salespeople jump right in to product or program benefits and features, without ever pausing to make sure the client is actually ready to listen to them.

4. Create consistency in your results. I have days where I'm on it. And days where I'm not. Last week I had a day where I was working on my book and happened to have a sales call in the middle of my writing time. So I jumped on, did a sloppy sales call, and guess what? They are probably not going to close. I KNOW the importance of the sales script and I still chose to wing it. And now, I get to reap those inconsistent rewards. I'm human. I'm not 100% focused every day. I'm not on top of my game all the time. And the benefit of the sales script is that it keeps my performance consistent, even when I am feeling inconsistent.

Sales Scripts are CRITICAL! And I hope you will seriously take the time to work on yours. Your business with thank you. So will your bank account.

I have many different sales scripts that I use in my business. But I learned years ago that asking people to write out their 7 essential sales scripts is a bit overwhelming. So, for this book, we are going to focus on 4 critical sales scripts.

1. FOCUS Intro

2. Your reach out script

3. Your Setter Script

4. Your one-on-one close

The FOCUS script is found in the next chapter. Because it's fairly short. It's easy to put together. And you'll use it ALL THE TIME!

The other three scripts are long. They require a good deal of explanation and training. And you're going to have to put some effort into customizing your templates. Those three are located in the Appendix. You can choose to work on your scripts now, or you can continue learning about general sales skills and then come back to them at the end. There is no sales scripting police to get in trouble with, so you choose what works best for you.

I debated writing an entire book on the anatomy of a sales script. And maybe someday I will. But for now, I'm asking for a little bit of trust and a go-with-the-flow attitude. I'm not going to get into all the explanations of every single piece of the sales scripts. Rather I'm going to give you a template and a little bit of guidance on how to customize it to fit your needs. Then go out and practice it. Don't skip steps or leave parts out because they seem unimportant. Each piece is incredibly important!

The Psychology of Sales

Before we jump into scripts I want to take a moment to talk about the psychology behind the sales script and give you some important tips.

I often get asked how I learned sales scripting. My degree is actually in linguistics and I have always loved language and communication. When I started taking sales courses my mind started dissecting the way people respond to certain phrasing -- How some phrases would cause the prospect to close off, and others would cause them to open up. So I would say my affinity for sales scripting is ⅓ a strange super power and ⅓ a study of traditional sales training and ⅓ tons and tons of practice.

Here are some good rules to remember about the psychology of sales.

1. You cannot sell to an overflowing mind. And most people's brains are overflowing.

People's brains are very full and overloaded. As a rule of thumb, most people you meet with will be kind of overwhelmed with their lives. They will feel like their plate is already full. And will oftentimes say no just so that they don't have to add one more thing in their life. Even if it is exactly what they have been looking for. Because of this, you've got to spend a good bit of time opening their minds, helping them see a need, and creating space before you give any information about your product.

2.   People need connection more than they need information.

We live in the information world. For a year, I was part of a little co-op where twelve families took turns milking a cow and taking care of our little homestead. We raised meat chickens and turkeys. And when the families got together on slaughter day, I was busy with work. So I had to go by myself to harvest ours. I was not looking forward to this. I don't particularly like killing anything. And I had no idea what I was doing. So I went online. I found a lady who made a Youtube video on how to kill your chickens peacefully. She taught me everything from how to thank my chickens for their life and nourishment and then kindly send them into the next realm, to the practical side of how to slit their throats and pluck their feathers. Between blogs and Youtube I found everything I needed to know. But I still really wanted someone to be there with me. Why? Because I was nervous and uncertain. I wanted to feel like someone knew what to do and had a plan. I wanted to be able to pull from an expert's confidence.

Now before you start sending me hate mail for killing chickens, I'll just say this. If we are going to each meat, I'd much rather know that they were well cared for, and that it's not pumped full of hormones and junk. So no, I'm not vegan. But no, I don't hate animals. And this is a perfect story to demonstrate my point.

If you are still trying to inform people into buying your products, please do everyone a favor and stop. They don't need you to educate them nearly as much as they need you to build a relationship of trust with them, and walk them through the decision-making process so they can feel good about their purchase.

3.   It is always better to ask questions than give statements.

I cannot stress enough the importance of asking questions. You will get so much farther in your sales if you ask questions and allow your client to claim what they want rather than trying to tell them what they want.

If I tell you the sky is pink, you are likely to disagree with me. But if I ask you, "Have you ever seen a pink sky?," your brain will automatically start thinking about whether or not that is true. For rule-based think-ers, you may still come up with a no. For people who are more fluid thinkers, you will probably come up with images of sunsets with beautiful oranges, pinks, and purples and may come back with the answer "yes." As a lover of all sunrises and sunsets I can attest, sometimes the sky is pink.

When you tell someone a statement, their inner voice either agrees or disagrees with you. Their inner voice is stronger than your voice. And if we are being honest with ourselves, our inner voice is not always right, logical, kind, or even helpful.

You can't inform someone out of that. What you can do is ask questions to help the person break through that negative, limiting inner voice, and really connect with what they want and need.

It is possible to ask questions to lead someone only towards the answer you want them to give. Every legal show on TV demonstrates this when the opposing counsel cries out, "Objection! Leading the witness."

That type of questioning can be manipulative. It is a VERY fine line between the type of questions that are manipulative and helpful. The questions often sound the same. The difference is really in your intention.

When I am selling, my goal is to get the client to the outcome that is best for them. Because I care for my clients in that way, they can feel it from me. Often times working with me is what is best for them, but not always. And when it's not right, I don't push it. I simply let it go!

Why talk about psychology when we are in a chapter about sales scripts?

Because a good sales script takes the client through a decision-making process. It's all about psychology.

You may wonder why a script follows the flow it follows. Or you may be tempted to change the order. I discourage that until you get to a point where you truly understand the psychology behind your script.

Here's what a good closing script should accomplish:

1. Reassure your potential client

2. Establish trust

3. Clarify where the client is at, where they want to be, and the gap between the two.

4. Identify need and desire

5. Increase hope for a solution

6. Get the client committed to making changes

7. Inform the client of your product or service

8. Allow the client to make a decision simply, and easily.

The scripts in the Appendix will make your investment in this book 100X what you paid for it.

Case Study

Mark is a veteran newscaster who stepped into media consulting and entrepreneurship about a year ago. And it was a struggle. He was working hard and talking to everyone he knew. But had experienced very little success. Frustrated and on the verge of throwing in the towel, we connected at an event and he became my client.

Within two months of working together, he went from zero clients, to closing his first three consulting contracts. Each were significant deals.

The two things we worked on were clarifying his offers, and writing his scripts. That was all he needed to go from no sales, to a good closing ratio. Every conversation he has now is productive. Not all of them close. But there is always interest, and his pipeline is effectively filling.

Make sure you visit the Appendix and spend some time there customizing your scripts!

Notes

CHAPTER 5:
Focus Intro

B ad intros are the worst. I cringe when I hear them. Here are some of my top offenders.

The Jack-of-All-Trades: "I'm Alex and I am a real estate agent, but I also do kids parties on the weekends, and I do some bookkeeping, oh, and bee-keeping."

Let's be honest here. Even if you are successful in all of these, it makes you sound like you are struggling or can't make up your mind, so you're trying out a bunch of things. Which is cool in your 20's. Try a lot of stuff, see what you love. But if you are a serious business owner/entrepreneur, an introduction like this does not leave me feeling confident in working with you.

The What?: "I help people align with their soul purpose and reconnect with their higher self so they can experience higher levels of healing and bliss in their relationships."

These type of introductions honestly leave the listener confused. You just explained what you do, and they still have no idea what you do. You'll hear things like, "So you're a preacher?" or "So do you do coaching?" Or worse yet, they won't even ask you to clarify because they don't want to sound dumb. Your intro isn't drawing people in. It's confusing them.

The Slow Down! This isn't a sales pitch: "I am the premier mortgage broker in the area, have you thought about buying or selling. The market's hot right now and I could get you the best rates out there. I'll even drop my fees if we can get something signed this week. When can we do lunch and discuss paperwork?"

You might think you are coming across as confident and powerful. You are actually coming across as pushy and insincere. Settle down, my friend. Take a breath. And let's try this again.

You need a powerful introduction that accomplishes the following:

- Clearly and concisely states what you do

- States who you help

- States the results you create

Here's a template for you to try out for yourself. Play with some different approaches and see what communicates best and sounds most authentically you.

I am a (Title)

I work with (Ideal Client)

Because most (3 pain points)

-

-

-

So I help (3 benefits)

◆

◆

◆

Bottom line (Bold statement of what you do)

****

Sample:

I am a small business consultant. I work with small business owners and entrepreneurs to scale and grow their business.

Because most

- ◆ Don't have consistent leads

- ◆ Are experiencing inconsistent cash flow

- ◆ And don't have a team because they don't think they can afford to hire

So I help them build a foundation for their business to run well by

- ◆ Getting them the right marketing strategy

- ◆ Building a sales system

- ◆ And teaching them how to start hiring the right people at the right price.

Bottom line: I take business owners from struggling to get it all done themselves and to running a profitable company that produces between 6 and 7 figures year after year.

Notes

CHAPTER 6:

Overcoming Objections

Overcoming sales objections is a critical skill. There are far too many people losing out on sales because they are just not confident with it.

Here's a good indicator that you might not be confident in overcoming objections. Someone says, "I love your product, but I just can't afford it right now." And your answer is, "Okay, I totally understand there's no pressure to buy anything. If I can't help you in anyway in the future, just let me know. Keep my number and if anything changes, give me a call."

Your job as a salesperson is to help determine the potential client's needs, find a product that fills that need, and then help them get out of their own way so they can actually get the things that they need.

The first thing to understand about objections is that they actually have very little to do with you or your product. These are their go-to excuses that stop them from getting what they want in all areas of their lives.

If a client tells you they can't afford their product, they are likely saying that for other things. If they tell you they don't have time, they probably say that often. I think this is important to understand because it will help you stay more objective rather than having an emotional response.

The second thing I want you to understand is that overcoming objections will not help you close people that aren't interested in your product. It will help you get to the hard no faster so you can move on. But it isn't a magic formula to take someone uninterested and make them interested. What it will do is help people that want your product or service feel more confident in saying yes. And it will get people off the fence who are being vague.

Here is the simple 4-step process is what I use to overcome every objection.

1. **Acknowledge the client's concern**. This is important. Have you ever given someone an objection like, "Well, I just don't have time right now?" And the salesperson responds with something like, "But if you did this right now I'll be able to throw in XYZ." Or you say, "I just can't afford it. It's not in the budget." And you get a response of, "No problem. You can just put it on your credit card."

How does that make you feel? Not really valued, a little annoyed and ready to end the sales conversation. So we're going to do it differently. We are going to acknowledge what they said by repeating it back to the client.

"Okay, so it sounds like you're interested in the product, but you're just not sure if now's the right time, is that accurate?" Easy breezy, right?

2. **Ask a Question**. The question will open doors inside of their mind to keep the conversation moving. So for example, if we got the objection of time, the conversation would sound like this.

"So what I'm hearing is you're interested, you're just not sure if this is the right time. Is that accurate? Yes. Okay. Well, can I ask you a question? If you were to do this now, what would be the benefits?"

Now the door is open again to conversation.

3. **Ask Permission to share information.** So many times when

salespeople are overcoming objections, it feels combative. It goes like this, the potential client gives an objection,the salesperson give them more information, the client gives another objection, salesperson gives them more information. It just feels very back and forth, and back and forth. It's aggressive, and it's competitive. And they may buy from you, but your return rates are going to be high, and they are likely to not buy from you again. So maybe you got the deal, but you lost the client. That's not what we want. We want to create a good, yummy environment where our clients love the experience of being sold to. So we acknowledge their objection, we ask the question to keep the conversation going and circle back around. Then we get permission so we can move on to step 4.

4. **Share information.** Give the client any information that will help them see a solution to their challenge. This is where you can talk about financing options or payment plans. This is where you can discuss case studies that will help build their confidence if they are being held up by a fear of failure.

Because we have taken time to get to this point, you will find your prospects much more open to hearing your information. They are more receptive and much more likely to close than when you try to battle them with your information.

The final thing to understand about objections is that they come in layers. Oftentimes the first objection the client gives you isn't really the main objection. The client might not even be fully aware of what is stopping them from saying yes. But as you overcome the first objection, it will help the client get more clear on what is really holding them back. I find that it's often the third objection that is the real hold-up.

Notes

CHAPTER 7:

Overcoming the Financial Objection

H ere's the deal with prospective clients telling you they can't afford your services: It actually has NOTHING to do with you, your product or your service. This is the same story that pops up for them all over the place. It's why they haven't taken the vacation they've been wanting to take. It's why they tell their kids no when they ask for things. It's their story.

STORIES ARE EXPENSIVE AND YOU CAN'T AFFORD TO BUY THEM!

There are really 3 reasons money might be an issue.

1. They are not financially qualified for your services, meaning they truly cannot afford to work with you and financing your product or services would be irresponsible for them.

2. They can pay if you will find a financing schedule that works for them.

3. They are a budgeter. They actually have the money, but hadn't allocated it for this purpose and would have to go back through the budget to make some changes.

Remember with overcoming objections, we are not trying to get them to buy things they don't need or want. We are trying to help our clients figure out how to get what they want.

That means you need to know if they are telling you they can't afford it because they are too nice to tell you they are not interested, or if they do want to work with you.

Here's how I figure that out.

Financial Objection Script:

So it sounds like money is the concern. May I ask you a question? If the money wasn't an issue and we could figure out financing, do you feel like this is the right option for you?

If they say yes:

Well, I would hate if money was the only thing that stopped you from getting (the outcome they are wanting). Do I have permission to brainstorm with you and see if we can find a way to make this work?

Now it's time to give your information. I love using questions in all of my scripting. Here are some ideas of how you could lead into informing the client of payment options or unique you have seen clients pay for your product or service.

- If you were going to purchase today, what ideas do you have for how you could get started?

- When you've purchased similar programs in the past, how did you finance them?

- Would it be helpful if we discussed financing options? (Only use this one if you have financing options)

- ◆ Do you have any areas you are currently spending on that would be replaced by this service/product?

I have found that it is MUCH more effective if the client is an active participant in brainstorming how they will pay for your service. So ask questions, get them thinking and then see what you can do to make it work for them.

If they say no, they don't feel like this is the right option for them:

Then you can ask what the real concern is.

One final word of caution. Don't just discount the program when they can't afford you. Discounted clients tend to be the biggest pain to work with and they seem to expect the most from you. If someone is truly not financially qualified, let them go and find someone who is a better fit.

Notes

CHAPTER 8:
Overcoming the Time Objection

Time can be a big hang-up for clients who are trying to make a decision. And time can be one of the more difficult objections you get.

Time shows up in a few different ways:

- I'm too busy right now
- It's not the right timing
- Call me back in a few months

- Can you just email me the details, I don't have time to get on a call

And I'm sure there are other ways it shows up. That's just a few I hear often.

I want to share a little bit of psychology behind the time objection before we get into the script.

Time is not actually the issue. We all have 24 hours in a day, 7 days in a week, and 365.25 days in a year. (I have to count the ¼ day because I am a leap year baby and that ¼ day adds up to one magical day once every 4 years for me.)

And in that time, we choose what is most important to us. We choose to put our time into maintaining our status quo life, or we put our time into building the life we want. We cannot make more time. We cannot borrow time. We cannot find time. We can only dedicate time.

I am incredibly busy. My schedule is jam-packed and if I'm being honest, this is probably my most commonly used objection. But, here's the deal -- when a solution comes up that can help me get closer to my goals, I do it. I dedicate time to the things that are the highest priority to me. Your clients are also dedicating time. Maybe not to their highest priority things. But they are still choosing where to spend that time.

Here are some of the realities behind a client claiming they don't have enough time:

- They are lacking in support, feel overwhelmed by their current load and are hesitant to take on anything else.

- They are disorganized, frantic, and worry they will fail.

- They are indecisive and think putting off the decision will somehow make it easier.

- They are afraid of success and failure and have been avoiding jumping all in to their dreams. Instead they keep it on the back burner and that lets them avoid any risk by staying in planning mode.

- What you are offering them is not as high of a priority as the things they are currently doing. (Warning: this one is not likely to close.)

Why does this matter? When you are learning how to overcome objections in sales, particularly the objection of time, you've got to understand that the real roadblock doesn't always have the same root. And when you are overcoming this objection, it's helpful to understand their situation a little bit more.

So here's how I script this one out.

Time Objection Script

1. Acknowledge the Objection: So it sounds like you are interested, but you (restate their time concern as they stated it, i.e. you're not sure it's the right time, you are too busy, etc.) Does that sound accurate?

2. Ask a Question: May I ask you a question? If we set aside timing for a minute, do you think this is the right program/product/service for you? And is time an issue in general in your life?

3. Ask Permission: Do I have permission to brainstorm with you and see if we can figure out a solution to the timing challenge? Because I know you want X now, but you don't have time to do what it takes to get you there. If you're open to brainstorming with me, I think we can come up with a plan.

4. Inform: I always love using questions to help people find their own answers rather than me telling them what I think. So here are some good questions that will help you see what type of Time challenge you are dealing with.

   a. If you were to take this on now, what would be your specific concerns? And what would be the benefits?

   b. If you don't take this on now, and a year from now everything is the same for you, would you be okay with that? Or would that be frustrating to you?

   c. Is there anything you are currently spending time on that isn't bringing you closer to your goals?

   d. What type of support would you need in order to be successful with this?

Bonus strategies: If they still need a little help saying yes, these two strategies work well with time.

Feel, Felt, Found: I know how you feel. When I was starting my business, I felt similarly. I was having my 5th son. I was overwhelmed with starting a new business. And it seemed like the worst time in the world to start a coaching program. But what I found was I really needed someone to save me time by just telling me what to do. Because my time was so limited, and my support was so minimal, I needed the fastest path to success. And I found that with hiring a great coach. Do you think that could be true for you as well?

The Green Light: (Name), can I be honest with you? It sounds to me like you want this, but you are trying to find the perfect moment. And in my experience, that doesn't really exist. If you were to drive to work tomorrow and not leave your house until you knew that every single light was green, would you ever get there? No. Sometimes, you just have to decide that you want it now, and take the red lights and green lights as they come. You make more progress than you would if you just kept waiting. So what do you think, are you willing to jump in?

Notes

CHAPTER 9:

Overcoming the Spouse Objection

Do you dread when you're having a sales conversation and some-body says, "Well, I'm gonna have to talk to my husband first?" Or "I need to run this past my wife?"

So let's talk about the psychology behind "I need to talk to my spouse." There are a few reasons why this comes up, and not all of them have to do with having a spouse that controls the purse strings.

Sometimes it's a personal trust issue. They don't trust themselves to make a good decision. Or maybe they really hate making decisions so they want other people to make the choice for them.

Or maybe they want to say no, but they don't feel like they have the ability to say no to you. It's easier for them to pass blame to their spouse, so their spouse can say no to you.

Or they like to let their spouse weigh in on important decisions.

Or it could be that they legitimately have a spouse who's going to have concerns with it.

Or it could be that they have a super controlling, super jerky spouse who never supports them in anything that they do.

The important thing to point out is that you have NO IDEA WHY the prospect is saying they have to talk to their spouse. Don't make assumptions. Don't make up stories. Stories are expensive, and you can't afford to buy them.

So the first thing that you can do to start moving past this objection is to change the story inside of your head from one of jumping to conclusion to a more productive habit of asking great questions.

To overcome this objection we are going to follow the 4 step process: acknowledge the objection, ask a question, get permission, give them more information.

Acknowledge: Okay, so what I'm hearing is that you want to do this, but you just need to run it by your spouse first?

If they if they were using the spouse as an excuse just to get off the hook of having to say no to you, they'll probably respond with something like, "Well, I'm not sure if I'm interested." And then you can address the real concern. But most of the time, they'll say, "Yeah, I just need to run it past my spouse.

Question: Okay, well, can I ask you a question? What do you think your spouse will say?

This will help you understand the nature of the real concern.

1. The spouse is probably going to say yes, but they just want to run it past them out of respect.

2. They think that their spouse is going to have serious concerns.

3. They think that their spouse is going to say straight up "No," and

they find it very unlikely that they're going to be able to progress the conversation.

It's important for me to know what they're walking into when they go and talk to their spouse so I can adjust the information I give them.

Permission: Do I have permission to brainstorm with you a little bit and give you some tips on how to present this to your spouse?

Information:

1.   Spouse that is likely to say yes:

Great! Let's go ahead and get all the paperwork filled out while we are here together to save both of us the time of needing to meet up again. And then I'll just wait to process it until after you've had a chance to talk with your spouse. Does that work for you?

2.   Spouse that will have concerns:

Do I have permission to throw an idea out there? What if the three of us got on a call? And we talked through this together so that way you aren't having to try to remember everything we talked about and pass on second-hand information? I can answer all of the questions that he/she has directly. Would that be helpful?

3.   Spouse that will probably say no:

I actually give them a simple script to use with their spouse. Here it is:

"I know you've probably noticed I've been struggling with X. I've been looking for resources and I've found one that has everything I'm looking for. I'll get help with

◆

◆

◆

It will cost $$. My plan to pay for it is _____.

I would like for you to support me in that."

I can't promise that the spouse will say yes, but this is a healthy way to start the conversation. Children ask their parents for permission. I've been married for 19 years and my husband and I are not on the same page 100% of the time. So we discuss until we come to an agreement. I don't ask my husband for permission, and he doesn't ask me for permission. But we frequently ask each other for support.

Notes

CHAPTER 10:

How to Sell to Indecisive People

They want it, they need it, but they just can't commit! It's tricky. I get it. We don't want to lose the sale by giving up too soon, but we also don't want to be strung along, missing out on other sales while we do everything in our power to get this person to sign.

The first key to selling to indecisive people is to recognize what type of indecisive person they are.

1. **People Pleaser**: People pleasers want to make everyone happy with them and have a very hard time saying no. Because they are taking your feelings into consideration, they have a hard time getting clear on what they want. You can sell to a people pleaser by

manipulation, but DON'T! You will have more cancellations and dissatisfied clients if you take this route, and both of those are expensive. Instead, use verbiage like, "It seems like you are having a hard time deciding. If you take me out of the picture, what would you most want to do? Because even though I would love to have you as a client, I wouldn't want you to decide to work with me unless it is absolutely what you want."

2. **Co-Dependent:** Co-dependent people struggle to make decisions on their own. They want someone else's input. Sometimes that other person really does need to be involved in the decision, and sometimes they have no business being involved in the decision. The key to selling to this type of person is to find out who the other person they need to talk to is. The second step is to ask, "Does this person play a role in (your business, your household management, your daily hair styling, etc.)?" If they do play a role and should be involved in the decision, simply ask, "Can we get them on the phone or schedule a time when the three of us can meet?" If they are not involved, ask the question, "What do you think they will say, and why is it important to you to talk to them first?" Honestly, I could write an entire chapter on how to close this one, but for the sake of keeping this chapter from becoming a novel we'll leave it at that. This will give you some crucial information to get the conversation started.

3. **Over-Analyzer:** This person needs a lot of details! They will want to read everything you have printed, they will want to interview your clients, they will want to scope out your website, and they may want to pull a background check on you. To sell to this type of person DO NOT ask them to make a decision before they know what they need to know. You will break rapport. Asking this type of person to act without information is like asking them to jump off a cliff when they don't know what is at the bottom. Instead, ask the questions: "What do you need to know in order to feel good about this purchase? What other questions can I answer for you? What type of information would you like on this?" They may need to read through information on their own, but whenever possible try to get all of their questions answered during your meeting. Make sure you set a follow-up call with a very firm date and time. Set the follow-up call for a day or two later. Don't let them go a week, because during that time they will come up with another question, not have an answer, and decide that it isn't going to work for them.

4. **Feeler:** Feelers need to feel good about the purchase and no amount of logic or information will replace their having an internal confirmation about what is right to do. These people will need to pray about it, sleep on it, consult their crystals, do muscle testing, or any other host of things that are completely unrelated to your conversation. Believe it or not, I am a feeler. I do get a lot of information and ask questions so I can see the big picture, but when it comes down to it, if I don't get a good vibe, I will not work with someone. But that is not the kiss of death! Feelers need an internal confirmation, but they can also get that pretty quickly. You just need to ask them questions that will get them looking inside right now. Use phrases like, "I understand and I want you to feel good about this decision too. Can I ask you a question? As we have gone through the information about (my product, service, etc.) what is your heart telling you? Are you feeling comfortable with me? Do you want a few minutes alone to check in and see if you feel like this is right?"

5. **Green Lighters:** This group wants the perfect time. They want the stars to align. They want all of the lights to be green before they start out. This is the most challenging group for me to work with. I will have people who really want to coach with me and just need to wait for the right time, and a year later they are saying the same thing, and again the next year, same conversation. It's crazy! Your goal with these people is to help them understand that if they choose not to move forward, they will not receive the benefits they are looking for. I do everything I can to close these people on the spot because I have found they are the least likely to close at a later date. I will ask them questions like, "Why does this feel like the wrong time?" What would need to happen for this to feel like the right time?" If they say something like, "The fall would be better," don't accept that answer! They are just trying to put off making the decision. However, if they have something concrete coming up, like they're having a baby in 3 weeks and it's not a good time ... you will want to accept that answer, it's legit!

All of us are indecisive at one point or another. Don't get frustrated with your clients, just patiently resolve their concerns. They are human and so are you! If you want to attract people who are more ready to make decisions, get clearer in your own decisions. Don't ask people to do what you are not doing. What brand of indecision shows up for you?

Notes

CHAPTER 11:
How to Sell to Difficult People

Ahhh, the Hecklers, the Know-It-Alls, and the Doubters. They are not our favorite people to sell to. I definitely prefer hearing, "This is exactly what I've been searching for!" But at every event you are going to have a tricky person to sell to. I know speakers and trainers who just let difficult people go and only work with the excited ones. You can do that. I also know that I have had some that were stinkers during the sales process and ended up being my most loyal and long-running clients. I've also closed stinkers who turned into stinker clients. The key is to know which ones you need to let go and which ones really need you.

Why are they stinkers?

Most human beings are good and it is in our nature to protect ourselves. When you come across crusty people, they are usually nursing some type of hurt. Hecklers have often been through rejection or ridicule and had to laugh their way out of it. Know-It-Alls often can't handle feeling weak and imperfect. And Doubters often have a history of being taken advantage of. The first step to handling a tough sale is to try to understand the person and think of them as a good person.

The Heckler: Makes jokes, derails the presentation, asks completely irrelevant questions, etc.

Remember that hecklers like to see you sweat. They like pushing buttons. The easiest way to handle a heckler is to get them on your side. Laugh with them. Joke with them. Understand that they want to be seen and heard, and treat them with kindness. When they like you, they will also sometimes be the most outspoken proponents of your products.

The Know-it-All: Everything is great in their life, they don't need help, every time you get close to finding their pain or problem they will block you

Know-It-Alls have a hard time showing weakness. They are usually strong and are used to doing things on their own. They do not want to feel incompetent or wrong. If you keep pushing to figure out their problems, they will put up wall after wall after wall. When I come across these situations, I pull back and invite them to tell me what they see that isn't working. If they come up with nothing, I ask them what they want that they don't have and then I ask permission to help them come up with solutions to get there.

The Doubter: Second-guess you and your product. Want proof. Treat you like you are trying to pull one over.

NEVER sell this person into a product or service, you have to let them choose into it. If you talk them into it, they will inevitably blame you for their life going all wrong! Ask them if they have had a negative experience before. Listen to them and ask questions like, "What do you need from me so that this is a different experience?" Keep asking them, "What else do you need to know before you can decide if this is right for you?" Give them any type of reassurance they ask for. If they want references, let them call your clients. If they want facts, show them where to find it. Your job in this situation is to inform anywhere they need it and continue to invite them to get more answers until they have no more questions. Then you ask for the sale.

Know when to RUN!

Anyone that has worked with a pain-in-the-butt client knows they make your life miserable. Some of my favorite clients and people have fit into these three categories in the beginning. But if they can't pass this test, I will not work with them. My test is simple. Can they take accountability for themselves, or do they blame others? If they blame others, they will blame me. If they can take accountability, I know we will be able to work together as soon as they are ready and I will move forward. If not, I bust out of that sales call as soon as possible!

Notes

CHAPTER 12:

Weird Sales Tricks that Work

I have been in sales for 20 years now. Wow that makes me feel old, but it also means I have a ton of experience under my belt! During the past 20 years, I have studied people, sales tips, strategies and techniques, and then studied people some more. I have learned that certain things work, and others don't. Today I want to share with you some of my weirdest sales tips! I can't fully explain the psychology behind why they work, but I can promise you that they do!

1. **Popcorn**: Popcorn works in live sales presentations. If you are a speaker, presenter, or network marketer, this one will be your best friend. I heard once that if you put popcorn kernels on the stove and apply heat, but remove them before they pop, that those

kernels can never be popped again. They had their moment, and the moment passed by. I haven't verified it. Part of me wants to see if it really works, and part of me doesn't because it would ruin my awesome analogy. Which is: as you apply heat to the popcorn kernels, for awhile nothing happens. Then all of the sudden you get your first pop! After that, the pops get closer together and pretty soon you have an explosion of awesome snackiness. People at live selling events work the same way. If you are selling to a group of people, you need to present a call to action to the group. If you do the call to action, but no one moves and you just end the event, you are not likely to close sales that night. However, if you will continue to talk and invite the audience into action until someone moves, you will close sales. You just need your first popper. Once the first person takes action, the others will follow. You know that awkward feeling at a gathering when it's time to eat and everyone wants it, but no one is going first? That is how your audience feels. Maintain the conversation until you get your first brave popper. You'll thank me for it!

2. **The Tunnel:** When I go into any sales experience, I visualize myself entering a tunnel. I will be in this tunnel for the entire conversation. At the end of the tunnel, my potential client can choose what direction they want to take. But during the conversation, we both have no way to move except forward. Here's why it works. How many times have you been in the sales conversation and wimped out, gotten off track, or stopped just short of asking for the sale? You can't do any of that in the tunnel, because there is no way to move except forward. This visualization keeps me extremely thorough in following my script and helps me dramatically increase my closing ratio.

3. **The Pen Pass:** This sales tip works any time you are trying to get someone to sign something. It could be at a vendor booth where you are trying to get them to enter your drawing. It could be that you are trying to get someone to sign a contract. You hold the pen for the entire conversation. Then, when it is time for you to get them to sign, instead of handing them the pen, set it on top of the paper in front of them. They actually sign at a much higher rate than if you hand them the pen directly.

4. **The Takeaway:** If you've ever been to a training with me, you know I am a little feisty. I learned this trick just because people annoyed me on my calls! Have you ever been in a sales conversa-

tion with someone and they are just impossible to talk with? They have all the answers, or they are full of doubt and reasons why something won't work for them? Well, in my early years I tried to convince them to work with me. I tried to talk them into liking me, my message, and my product. Then I decided I just didn't care about winning everyone over. So I started taking my offer off the table. Guess what happened? Those calls ended up going better! I'm not going to say I close them all, but there is something about knowing the services you need are about to be taken away that causes people to actually listen to what you have to say.

5. **The BFF:** This one is also a lesson I learned early on. I was trying to be so professional so I would be taken seriously! My knowledge of my products was perfect. My presentation was solid. But I just wasn't closing because I wasn't relatable. Now I go into every conversation thinking about that person as someone I have known forever. They are my BFF for the next hour and I have no one to impress. I can just go in and share my knowledge.

Notes

CHAPTER 13:
Always Know Your Numbers

This is the chapter you will be most tempted to skip. Fight the urge, my friends. You need this chapter!

We've all heard the saying that sales is a numbers game. But most people take that to mean, "You have to ask a bunch of people to get someone that will say yes."

Sure, that's partially true. But I want you to understand that your numbers will tell you EVERYTHING that is going on in your business. It's your diagnostics. And if you aren't looking at those numbers, it's like that crazy Netflix movie where Sandra Bullock drives her car blindfolded. (Full disclosure, I've never seen the movie, but people! That's some crazy stuff right there!)

When you know your numbers, your business becomes predictable. You know exactly what activities you need to do to hit a sales goal. And if business ever dips, you can go into your numbers and find quickly what is wrong.

Here are some must-know numbers:

Leads to Set Leads: How many of your total leads set up an appointment for a sales conversation with you?

You figure this out by dividing the total number of leads by the number of people you set.

If Leads to Set Leads is low, here's what I look at:

1. Marketing problem- Am I attracting the wrong leads?

2. Marketing problem- Are my leads needing more nurture and relationship building?

3. Reach-Out Problem- Do I need a different reach out approach?

4. Script Problem- Is my initial reach-out script bad?

Call Volume: This is the total number of sales calls made in a week.

If your *Call Volume* is low, the person making the calls is lazy or too chatty. They need some training and accountability check-ins to get them up to standard.

Calls to Sets: How many phone calls do you have to make before you schedule a sales call.

You figure this out by dividing the number of calls made by the number of appointments scheduled.

1. If Calls to Sets is low, here's what I look at:

2. Are my setters calling at the right times of day?

3. Are my setters being honest about their call volume?

4. Setter performance- Is the setter following the sales script?

5. Setter Performance- Is the setter able to connect with my clients and leave a good first impression?

Setter performance- Is the setter motivated to get results, or just dialing without concern of outcome?

Sets to Holds: How many appointments do you need to set to get one to hold?

You figure this out by dividing the number of appointments actually held by the number of appointments scheduled.

If *Sets to Holds* is low, here's what I look at:

1. Is my setter trying to work the system? Often times setters are compensated on their performance. I give mine set volume bonuses. Are they just going after the bonuses and not caring if the sets actually hold?

2. Is a commitment statement being used?

3. Are reminders being sent?

Percentage of Unqualified Sets: How many people do you get on a closing call with and then realize they were not qualified and shouldn't have been set in the first place?

You figure this out by dividing the number of unqualified sets by the total number of sets.

If Percentage of Unqualified Sets gets too high, here's what I look at:

1. Who is sending me the unqualified sets?

2. Do they need more training?

3. What did the client say that made the setter (or me) think they were more qualified than they actually were?

Calls to Closes: How many people that you held closing calls with closed on a program or service?

You figure it out by dividing the number of sales calls held by the number of new clients.

If *Calls to Closes* is low, that is an indicator that the person closing is struggling with their skills. They may need more training, or they might not be the right fit. It could also be an indicator that you are attracting the wrong type of leads and need to adjust your marketing. Having more than one closer help you to tell which is the case. If you have one closer that is selling well, and the other one is struggling it would be a sign that the skill level is the issue. If everyone is struggling across the board, it could be a lead source issue.

Average $ Amount per Sale: This is the average amount of money a new client spends with you.

You figure it out by dividing the total dollars sold by the number of new clients.

If *Average $ Amount per Sale* is low, that is usually an indicator that whoever is closing is uncomfortable going after the bigger deals. I recommend working your way up gradually. If you're currently closing $200 deals, don't just assume you're going to close 20K deals. Instead, shoot for a gradual increase in this number every month.

Total Sales: You should know how much you've sold for the week, for the month, the quarter and for the year. I know your official reports might not update that quickly, but you should keep a running total to give you an idea of where you are for the month.

This number will never be low on it's own. The way you solve this challenge is to look at all of the other indicators and see which ones are contributing to low total sales.

Phew. You made it! I know that chapter felt like reading a math textbook. And I'm proud of you for making it through, because it is truly one of the most important chapters in this whole book. Knowing your numbers is what sets apart the mom-and-pop shop from the company that scales for growth.

Start tracking! It doesn't have to be fancy. You could honestly set up a Google drive and just start entering your numbers each day.

You may find that you track things slightly differently. That's okay. Start with the numbers I track and as you realize one is irrelevant in your system, or you need something different, feel free to make those adjustments.

But start tracking! Not knowing your numbers is, quite frankly, a very risky and alarming way to run a business. I promise that your fear of numbers is not as scary as your business going under because you didn't see major problems. Your numbers will always tell you where the problems are! Listen to them, use them, love them!

Notes

CHAPTER 14:
Where Marketing and Sales Intersect

I would like to make a public service announcement. Sales is not marketing, and marketing is not sales! I can't tell you how often those terms get used interchangeably by the business owners I speak to. It wouldn't be a big deal if it was just words. But that represents two very separate departments in your company. And if you don't get them straight, you won't know where to adjust when you have a problem.

Think of it like this. What if you went to a doctor for chest pains, and they believed that the heart and lungs were basically the same general thing. So to fix your chest pains, he decides to do lung surgery. BIG problem, right?

The same thing happens in your business! I can't tell you how many times I've heard a company say they have problems with sales, but when we get into the numbers, their problem is actually in marketing. Or vice versa.

Let's get these straight!

Marketing is lead capture and lead nurture.

Sales is lead conversion.

Example one: Most businesses can and should be generating leads online. But some businesses don't sell well online. Their product or price point requires an in-person experience, demonstration or a personal conversation. When the business owner lumps sales and marketing together, they may think, "My business just doesn't work online." And they would miss out on all the potential for online growth.

Example two: A company is struggling with low sales numbers, so the owner assumes they have a problem in sales. They hire another salesperson. They play around with their price points. They are stressed about how to get more sales. But when we dig into the numbers, they actually have a good conversion ratio for their industry. They just REALLY underestimated how many leads they would need to reach their sales goals. If they don't separate out marketing and deal with it independently, they'll spend time, energy and money fixing things that were never broken.

Example three: A company is successful at generating an online following and can't understand why the thousands of likes, shares, and fans aren't turning into sales. They have made the big mistake of thinking blasting their info to the world counts as marketing and sales. It doesn't. They haven't taken the time yet to build an online sales funnel that matches their online audience.

When you group marketing and sales together, your business comes out the loser! Each department is an invaluable piece of your business. Each department deserves individual focus and attention!

Notes

CONCLUSION:
Practice Makes Perfect

Learning to love sales has been a journey for me! From my days of inadvertently hitting on girls in the mall to having the insight to write a sales manual for people who don't "naturally" sell, it's been quite the ride. And it's likely to be a journey for you as well.

Let me be 100% transparent on this important fact. It's going to take time and a lot of practice before you master these skills.

The first time you use a new script, it feels awkward. The first time you overcome an objection, it feels awkward. The first time you use a money declaration, it feels awkward.

One of my mantras is that life begins at the edge of your comfort zone.

Sales won't feel comfortable in the beginning. The first time I ran my bow across the strings of my cello, it was uncomfortable and it sounded just awful. Now when I play it's like catching up with an old friend and we fall right back into our rhythm. The confidence came with years of lessons, great teachers, practice and daily effort.

In Chapter 2 we talked about Skillset, Mindset, and Activity. This book has given you a lot of tools for your skillset and some great mindset tips. But the one thing it can't give you is the activity. You've got to get out there and start having sales conversations.

Find your driving desire

The only kids I've ever met that say, "I want to be in sales when I grow up," are the children of great salespeople. I happen to have one son who claimed he wanted to run the family business when he was about 8. He thought he would be great at sales and also that he could boss his older brothers around. So it sounded like a great plan to him.

But if you're like me, sales was probably pretty far from your mind when you were a kid, dreaming of what your adult life would be like.

When I got started in sales, I viewed it as a means to an end. It was something that had to be done. And I remember feeling like if it wasn't for sales getting in the way, I could help so many more people.

Now I realize that sales is the door that I open to allow all the people that need my help to come in. I love opening that door.

That shift from resentment into enjoyment came through practice, through finding scripts and languaging that worked well for me, and also through connecting with my driving desire.

The direct sales industry is really driven by prizes, recognition, and rank advancement. When I first started, I set all of my goals according to those three things. I would pick a prize and work towards it. Put the next rank on my goal poster and work towards it. I had some vague idea of success and free cars at the end of it. But that didn't really motivate me to get out there and sell when I didn't feel like it. It wasn't enough to cause me to get back into the ring after a disappointing blow.

A couple of years into my business journey I attended a John C. Maxwell value training and realized that money, recognition, and stuff were not in my top 5 values. At that time, money wasn't even in my top 10.

I truthfully can't remember what my top 5 values were. But I can tell you the things I value most now are family, lifestyle, living in alignment with my values, impact, influence, and having choices. As a result, I've always struggled to work for prizes or short-term wins.

If you are motivated by those things, that's awesome! Run with it. Go climb that rank ladder. Don't tone down your ambition to make anyone else comfortable. I know it's not the prizes that matter to you, it's the feeling you get each time you set out to achieve something and did it. The prizes are just the proof. Plus they are fun!

But for those of you that feel like you struggle to find your motivation, I give you permission to look internally rather than just shooting for the next thing.

In the end, the thing that motivated me was the idea of working with my husband and buying a property to raise our boys on. It was an awesome dream, and an even more beautiful reality. And that dream motivated me for years until we achieved it together.

If having ten acres and raising goats doesn't motivate you, that's cool.

The key is to find what does motivate you. What truly makes you tick? What dream can you get so excited about that you are willing to make calls every single day, whether you're feeling it or not?

Discipline vs. Passion

Passion is great. I love when I feel passionate about my business. But you know what? I don't feel it 100% of the time.

Guess what else I don't feel passionate about 100% of the time? EVERYTHING!

I love my family dearly. But after 19 years of marriage, there are days when I'm not feeling the passion. After 17 years of being a mother, there are days when I'm not feeling the passion.

On those days, I operate from discipline and commitment. I still take care of my kids. I still pray with my husband. I still squeeze his hand right before we go to sleep. Because I know that if I move forward in discipline the passion will come back. It always does.

You may experience days where you feel unmotivated and lack passion. Guess what? Do it anyway.

You may experience longer seasons when you lack passion. When it's been months or years since you felt passion and you've been going through the motions forever, I recommend it's time for a change. That doesn't mean you have to quit your business. But it does mean you need to give yourself permission to do it differently.

It's funny to me how quickly people are to give up when they lose passion for a day or a week, but how unwilling they are to change when the passion has been gone for years.

The best success happens in the middle. Passion will ebb and flow naturally. You don't have to feel it every day. But you should expect to feel it semi-regularly.

Sales can unlock your dreams

I live an incredibly blessed life. And I do not attribute that all to my skills. Building this life and this business has been a partnership with God. We've received so many opportunities and blessings along the way.

But I do want to say one thing. Sometimes the blessing and opportunity you've been looking for comes to you and it looks like work!

For me, all of my dreams started coming true when I finally learned to sell. It was like I'd been in a glass jar. I could see all of the possibilities around me, but I could never seem to access it. When I learned to sell it was as though the lid was unscrewed and I was free to pursue all of the abundance that I had seen everyone else participating in.

If you want it, then it's available to you. And may I suggest that you spend some time on your knees asking for the things you want. And then get on your feet and get to work.

I look forward to you living the life you've always dreamed of.

Appendix 1:
Reach-Out Scripts

When you are reaching out to for the first time to prospective clients, understand that it's just a numbers game. Some people will be annoyed you reached out, some will simply not respond at all. But you WILL find people that are interested. It takes patience on your part. And it takes a good reach-out script.

Social media has made reaching out to people easier than ever before. For example, if you are using Linked In, you can get on sales navigator and research everyone in their database that is your ideal client and it will give you a list to start your reach-outs. This is both good and bad.

It's good because it's easy to reach out. It's bad because, as consumers, we are all inundated with connection requests and cold reach-outs and it's getting old fast. There are a lot of strategies for these types of reach-outs. Here's what I've found does NOT work:

1. Vague requests to meet and see how we can support each other.

2. Bait and switch. You pretend like you are interested in their stuff, but really just want to pitch them on your services.

3. Long detailed emails that go over the details of what you do.

4. Really catchy personal connection emails to get the reader's attention. I actually like these reach-out and I wish they worked. The problem is, we are getting way too many reach-outs, so people are just not taking the time to read them.

Here's what I've found is working well right now; being short, sweet, and to the point.

Here are a few different templates depending on how you are reaching out.

Email Reachout:

Hi (Name)

(Use data mining to share something they have done that caught your attention i.e, I watched your video, read your article, saw your... and compliment them.)

I am reaching out because I (Focus Intro)

And I wanted to see if I could get 10 minutes of your time to see if I could

◆ Benefit

◆ Benefit

◆ Benefit

So what do you think? Do you have 10 minutes for me to ask you a couple of questions and see if I can (restate benefits)?

Thanks,

Name

Super signature

Can I help you with X (Include link)

Here's a great article (Include a link)

Here's something you might want to read (Include link)

Example:

Hi Dan,

I listened to your podcast on why every business needs a sales team. And it was fantastic.

I'm reaching out because I am a small business consultant. I work with small business owners and entrepreneurs to scale and grow their business. Because most don't have consistent leads, are experiencing inconsistent cash flow, and don't have a team because they don't think they can afford to hire.

So I help them build a foundation for their business to run well by

Getting them the right marketing strategy

Building a sales system

And teaching them how to start hiring the right people at the right price.

Bottom line, I take business owners from struggling to get it all done themselves and into running a profitable company that produces between 6 and 7 figures year after year.

And I wanted to see if I could get 10 minutes of your time to see if I could add value to your podcast audience by showing them how to hire a great salesperson, what they need in place before they hire, and how to get their sales people closing quickly after training.

So what do you think? Do you have 10 minutes for me to chat and see if I can be your next great interview for your show?

Thanks,

Amy

Phone Call to Individual:

Hi (Name)

Have I caught you at a good time or are you busy with family/clients?

Great, well I am calling because I (Focus Intro)

And I wanted to see if I could get 10 minutes to see if I could

+ Benefit

+ Benefit

+ Benefit

So what do you think? Do you have 10 minutes for me to ask you a couple of questions and see if I can (restate benefits).

The goal of these questions is to draw out a need, give them a couple of ways that you could help them and then invite them to schedule a longer pitch meeting.

Example:

Hi Elizabeth,

Have I caught you at a good time or are you busy with clients?

Great! Well I'm calling because I am a small business consultant. I work with small business owners and entrepreneurs to scale and grow their business. Because most don't have consistent leads, are experiencing inconsistent cash flow, and don't have a team because they don't think they can afford to hire.

So I help them build a foundation for their business to run well by

+ Getting them the right marketing strategy

+ Building a sales system

+ And teaching them how to start hiring the right people at the right price.

Bottom line, I take business owners from struggling to get it all done themselves and into running a profitable company that produces between 6 and 7 figures year after year.

And I wanted to see if I could get 10 minutes to see if I could

- Help you get more leads in the next 30 days
- Save money on your current marketing
- Convert more clients into your high-end programs.

So what do you think? Do you have 10 minutes for me to ask you a couple of questions and see if I can improve your marketing and sales?

Great!

Are you currently looking for more qualified leads?

Do you have anything you are spending on for marketing that isn't really producing for you?

If I could review your sales and marketing plan, and map out an improved strategy to get you more leads, and protect your budget would that be helpful?

Great. Let's go ahead and set that up.

Call to an Organization

Often when you call an organization, you don't know exactly who you need to speak with. So you can't just call the person you want on the first attempt -- you might be pitching to the secretary. Here's what I have found works the best to get you on the phone with the right person.

Call 1: The secretary:

Hi (repeat their name), I was hoping you could point me in the right direction. I'm (explain what you are doing) and I was wondering who is over (the department you need to work with).

(Get the name). Great. And would you mind giving me their extension/email?

I really appreciate your help and I hope you have a great day.

Call 2: The point person:

Hi (Name),

I was directed to you by (secretary's name) and told you are the person to talk to! How's your day going?

Great, well I am calling because I (Focus Intro)

And I wanted to see if I could get 10 minutes to see if I could

◆ Benefit

◆ Benefit

◆ Benefit

So what do you think? Do you have 10 minutes for me to ask you a couple of questions and see if I can (restate benefits)?

The goal of these questions is to draw out a need, give them a couple of ways that you could help them and then invite them to schedule a longer pitch meeting.

Example:

Hi Elizabeth,

I was directed to you by Patty from HR and she told me you are the person to talk to! How's your day going?

Great. Well I'm calling because I am a small business consultant. I work with small business owners and entrepreneurs to scale and grow their business. Because most don't have consistent leads, are experiencing inconsistent cash flow, and don't have a team because they don't think they can afford to hire.

So I help them build a foundation for their business to run well by

◆ Getting them the right marketing strategy

◆ Building a sales system

◆ And teaching them how to start hiring the right people at the right price.

Bottom line, I take business owners from struggling to get it all done themselves and into running a profitable company that produces between 6 and 7 figures year after year.

And I wanted to see if I could get 10 minutes to see if I could

◆ Help you get more leads in the next 30 days

◆ Save money on your current marketing

- Convert more clients into your high end programs?

So what do you think? Do you have 10 minutes for me to ask you a couple of questions and see if I can improve your marketing and sales?

Great!

Are you currently looking for more qualified leads?

Do you have anything you are spending on for marketing that isn't really producing for you?

If I could review your sales and marketing plan, map out an improved strategy to get you more leads, and protect your budget would that be helpful?

Great. Let's go ahead and set that up.

Appendix 2:
Qualifying/Setter Script

❧

The qualifying/setter script should be used with every lead that makes it to a certain point in your sales system. And that point should be predetermined by you.

For my first five years in business, I had a team of setters that literally called every single lead we got into the business. It didn't matter if they were warm or not, we called. Those calls allowed us to grow company sales VERY quickly. In my opinion, there are only two reasons you wouldn't want to use a setter script with every single lead. 1 - You have great funnels that bring in more leads than you can call and also convert on the less-expensive programs, or 2 - You don't want new clients.

This setter script can be used by the same person doing the high-ticket sales script. Or it can be a different person. I'll be honest, I don't love doing the dials, but I can close like nobody's business. I don't have the patience for making 100 phone calls a day. And some of my best setters have been amazing at doing the dials, but lacked the skill to be a great closer. So deciding whether you should have two separate people fulfilling these roles depends on the talent and work ethic of the people involved.

Qualifying/Setter Script

Hi, may I speak with (Name).

Hi (Name), this is _____ with (Company). You recently (State the lead source, i.e. registered for my ebook, attended our webinar, visited our vendor booth.)

State the connection so they know who you are, then ask a question that requires a conversational response.

The reason I'm calling is that as a follow up to the event, (Your company) is offering some additional support in the form of a one-on-one strategy session. It is a great opportunity to (State the benefits). I wanted to reach out to you and see if that is something that would make sense for you and if you're interested. How does that sound?

Here are the typical objections I get at this point, and what I say. Feel free to update and insert your own.

- **How much does it cost?** Nothing. This is an opportunity to get to know (Company/Product), how it works, and specifically what it does to help businesses/people like you.

- **It sounds interesting,** but I don't have time right now. I totally understand. This call takes about 10-15 minutes. Do you have that much time now or should I call back?

- **I don't know anything about your company/product or I haven't watched the webinar, etc**. That's not a problem. I'd still like to get to know you and a little about your business. If things match up, we can schedule this more tailored call and give you the opportunity to ask specific questions about your needs.

- **I don't have a business**. Oh, that's interesting. What brought you to (Lead Source)? Find out if they are looking to start a business. If not, politely end the call.

- **I am just too busy to do anything at this point.** I understand. Can I ask, what is your ideal timing for building your business and maybe even education?

  ◇ 1-2 months out: You know, if you're looking at business development or education, we're actually in the perfect time. It takes a while to get on the calendar and then actually the classes usually fill up ahead of time. So if we're talking that close we should schedule the coaching appointment now.

  ◇ 2-5 months out: Really, what's going on that you want to wait that long? Are you okay with keeping your business in status quo until then or is that when you're planning on really rocking your business? If you want to be rocking by that time, you might want to consider education and preparation now. (Walk them backwards through timing).

  ◇ 6+ months: I'm curious. Are you not really interested in business development or is something going to change between now and then? (Listen and if they're just not interested, let them tell you if they want to just go into a holding pattern with follow up every 3 months or so or if they just want off our list.)

- I just don't have any money. That's interesting. I'd hate to stop our conversation at this point since we're talking about a complimentary session. If it's okay, can we still go a little deeper and see if this is something that makes sense now or even later down the road?

First I will develop a quick profile with you to see where you are at with *(Your area of expertise, i.e. health, business, relationships.)* Then we can get you set up for the additional coaching.

Does that sound good? Great, let's get started.

Insert relevant qualifying questions. I ask questions that fit into these 4 categories.

- **Demographics:** Are they your ideal client? For me this has to do with size and phase of business.

- **Need:** Do they have a need that I can help them with? For example, if they need a website developer and that is their only need, I can't help them even if they are my ideal client.

- **Commitment to solving the problem:** Are they committed to working on the problem? I don't progress the conversation if they are not actually wanting to grow their business. If they are completely happy where they are, I'm completely happy to let them stay there.

- **Financial:** We need to know if the client is financially qualified. Can they afford your products or services? Trying to sell to someone that truly cannot afford your services is discouraging and a waste of time.

Verbiage to help with financial and commitment qualification:

Now let's talk about the resources you have for (your solution, i.e. business development, investing in your health, strengthening relationships.)

To get new results in your life, you need to do things differently. One of the biggest mistakes we see people make is wanting their life to change, but not being willing to sacrifice time, effort or money.

Are you willing to invest time into gaining new education and skills? And how much time per week are you willing to invest in your education? Are you ready to start a coaching program within the next 3 months?

And are you willing to invest money into gaining new education and new skills

And how much are you willing to invest in your education?

If they don't give you a number: We have multiple programs at multiple price points with the intention to find the right program at the right price for each person we speak to. I just want to make sure I refer you in the direction of a program that meets your current needs and makes sense financially. Can you give me an idea of how much funds you have available for (insert your service)?

On a scale of 1-10, how committed are you to (*the result they want, i.e. growing your business this year, your weight loss journey, getting out of debt*)?

Clearly state your qualifications so you or your setter can measure their responses and see if this lead is qualified.

1.

2.

3.

4.

5.

If they are qualified:

Based on what you have told me, I would love to offer you the one-on-one appointment to coach with (Insert Closer's Name). Let's go ahead and get you set up.

What works better for you, day time or evenings? And would you prefer beginning of the week or end of the week? How about _____ at _____?

Perfect. I am very excited for you to be able to experience coaching with our team. Because of the limited space for these strategy sessions, I just need a final commitment from you that you will be there, ready to learn. (Let them say they are committed). Sounds great, I will send you my (send something of value to help them get more acquainted with you) so you can get to know me a little bit better and I'll send you a confirmation email with all of the details of your session.

If they are unqualified:

Based on what I am hearing today, I think this strategy session is probably not the right fit for you. That session focuses on advanced (insert your strategies), and it sounds like we can best support you by helping you get the foundational pieces working first.

Offer your downsell, low-cost product, or free resources.

Appendix 3:
High-Ticket Sales Script

I tell all of my clients that the individual script is like an accordian. You need to go through all of the parts of the script. But if you are selling a lower-cost product, you can shorten every section and contract the script. If you want to sell a million dollar deal, you may expand this script over several meetings.

But this high-ticket script works well as is for anything from $100 to $100,000. It's pretty versatile. This script is written as a two-step close. If you are using a one-step close, you would just add the reach-out and the qualifying questions to the beginning of this script.

Section 1: Rapport and establishing need

Introduction: Setting the expectations for the call is critical. You are planting the seeds at the very beginning of the conversation that you have something to offer them. Let's be honest, the prospective client knows you are going to offer something and it is much less nerve-racking if you just tell them what is going to happen and when the offer is coming.

Greeting:

Set the stage for the sale:

1. Service objective

2. Result you will create

3. Let them know a pitch is coming

It might sound like this: *Hi Mike, It's Amy from Amy Walker Consulting. I'm looking forward to our call today. I'm going to focus on three things today. First, I'll ask you a lot of questions to help identify any challenges or needs in your company. Second, I'll map out an action plan and give you my recommendations. And third, if it looks like I could be a fit for you, I'd love to introduce you to my Mastermind Program. Does that sound good?*

Great, let's jump in.

Deeper-level Assessment Questions: Ask specific questions to draw out a client need as it relates to your services or products. For example, as a small-business strategist, I often ask about their sales, marketing, team, and if they are growing, stagnant or declining. If you were a fitness coach, you might want to ask about their energy levels, weight loss goals, what made them decide to make a change now, what they've tried in the past that either worked or didn't work, or even their diet. Determine your Assessment Questions.

1.

2.

3.

4.

5.

6.

Big Picture: Now I want you to take a step back, look at the big picture and tell me, what do you see is the problem?

The Client has been looking at their business under a microscope with the first questions. Now we want them to take a more comprehensive look and tell us what they think is the issue. This will oftentimes pull out their biggest concern or pain point. Sometimes they hit the nail on the head and are very accurate. Sometimes they tell me a Big Picture Assessment and they are not even close to what I see as the problem. Either way I agree with them. Why? Because it's what THEY see as the problem. It is real for them. And if I disagree with their truth, it breaks rapport and they question me. They don't feel like I understand their problem. If I agree with them and then say, "I can see that, and can I also add that I am seeing X is also an issue." They are much more receptive to hearing what I think is the problem.

Not working: I've definitely got some notes for your action steps, but I want to make sure we aren't missing anything. I'd love to go a little bit deeper and start analyzing what you are seeing is not working.

What do you see is not working with X?

Can you tell me more about that?

And what about Y? What isn't working with Y?

Are there any other challenges we haven't talked about but should have?

Section 2: Solution

The Solution: In this phase of the script, we are starting to go into how we can help them. DO NOT START COACHING THE CLIENT. Trust me, it kills the sale. The client feels like they just got so much information from you that they are going to have to spend the next few months working on it before they can get started working with you. Instead, I give them 4 Action Steps that are, what I call: The what, not the how!

Here's an example:

What	How

The first step is going to be to put together a comprehensive marketing strategy.	I think we should have you launch a podcast ,start pitching yourself for speaking gigs ,beef up your social media ,and run Facebook Ads.
Next I want you to build a sales system	You'll need to get all of your sales scripts written ,build out your system ,and start holding consistent sales calls.

Do you see the difference? The "what" is more of the big picture of how are you going to solve their problem. The "how" is the actual action steps you will take to get them there. The "how" is showing them the plan, opening up your playbook and giving them so much information that they think they can do it without you. Let's be honest, they can't. It might sounds simple enough to put together a comprehensive marketing strategy, but if they couldn't do it before, they still can't do it after 30 minutes on the phone with me. They need to work with me. I'm not keeping the "how" a secret. If someone is very detail-oriented, I'll give them glimpses into the how. But I am still very, very careful not to make them feel like I just told them everything they need to know.

Your "What" Action Steps:

1.

2.

3.

4.

Section 3: Commitment and Close

Commitment Process: This is where we shift gears and start getting the potential client to commit to change. Committing the client to fix their problem before you introduce them to your product or service is really important. If the potential client is not committed to change, they will not be closable. Why would they spend time and money to buy something to fix a problem when they don't really care if it gets fixed?

The other thing we are going to accomplish in this section is to help the client position the value. Too many people shop for solutions based on the cost of the program. "It's cheap, great I'll do it," or "Ohh, that's expensive, I'm going to have to say no." It's not a very wise way to shop for solutions. And it's the reason so many of us have spent money on solutions that don't work. So instead we are going to reposition the value. We want them to focus on the cost of the problem and the value of the solution.

"Alright, we are going to shift directions right now and the next questions I am going to ask you might be a little bit uncomfortable. Is that okay?"

How long has this been an issue?

What is it costing you?

(Ask for specifics: relationships, energy, peace of mind, and MONEY. Help them see that it is costing them to stay where they are.)

(Talk to me about ... Use this phrase to get them talking even more).

If we could solve these challenges and get (go over 4 Action Steps) working, what would that be worth to you?

What would you gain by solving these challenges?

Close: It sounds like you have a lot of reasons why you need to do this. Are you committed? (Listen to what they say and then ask a follow-up commitment question). And are you committed to making the sacrifices it will take to get you there?

Introduce your program, product, or service:

Would it be okay if I tell you how my program could help you with that?

Give the Program Details: Focus on benefits and outcome more than deliverables. I am always tempted here to just give them a long list of all the things I'll do for them. But it's not as effective as presenting your program features with a benefit statement.

Here's an example:

Feature: You can submit questions to me through Marco Polo.

Benefit: Get ongoing support as you are working on your business through daily video coaching.

List your Program Details:

-
-
-
-
-
-

So what do you think? Would you like to work with me?

If no: May I ask why? (Overcome objections- go back to those chapters if you need a refresher)

If **"Well how much does it cost"**: We can definitely go over cost and I promise I will do everything I can to help you figure out how to be in the program if it is what you want, but first I have to know if it is even what you want. Because I would hate if money was the thing that stopped you from getting _____. So do you want this?

Guys, this wording is pretty magical. I want my prospective clients to claim if they want to work with me. Once they say yes, it changes something in their mind. They have claimed what they want and they are much more likely to say yes once we talk money.

Start up details: Give any relevant on boarding details, like start dates for when you can work on their project, dates and locations for an upcoming event, how soon they can begin the digital course, etc.

-
-
-
-

Now, let's talk about finances.

- Price

- Payment options: Visa, MC and American Express. How would you like me to process your registration?

How does that sound?

Overcoming objections: You learned about this in previous chapters. Make sure you write out what your most common objections are so you can be prepared to overcome them.

- Money

- Time

- Trust

- Permission

Finalize the sale: Once you get the yes!

I am so excited for you! This is a great decision and I know you will (state key benefit).

Now that you have decided you want to do this, let's go through what your next steps look like.

First we need to finalize your payments. (Get the details of the plan, read it back to them.) Does that sound good? Perfect! I will go ahead and submit that right now.

Second, I'll send you the agreement and we can review that quickly. (Go over what is included in the program and also what is expected of you the client.)

Tips for Study Groups or Book Clubs

Are you part of a sales team? The "I'm not a salesperson" Sales book is perfect to use for your next study group or book club.

How to host a sales team book club:

1. Set a start date and have all members get the book before you launch.

2. Set a time each week to meet in person or via zoom.

3. Read and discuss one chapter each week.

4. Assign power partners within the group so everyone has someone to practice with and keep them accountable.

5. Schedule Amy to speak to your book club. For groups under 50, Amy will send you a video to encourage your sales team and answer their questions. For groups over 50, Amy will do a live virtual session. If you wish to have Amy come train your team in person, please reach out for pricing. amy@amywalkerconsulting.com Subject: Sales Book Club or Sales Training.

Questions for your discussion:

1. What success tips did you gain from your reading this week?

2. How did that make a difference in your activity and results this week?

3. Did you encounter fear or resistance as you were making changes in sales efforts?

4. What did you do to strengthen your sales mindset this week?

5. How did your sales skill set improve this week?

6. How did your sales activity improve this week?

7. Leave time for questions and role play! (Those are the most important part!)

Attend a Live Event

Want to meet Amy in person, and get some serious sales and marketing training? Now's your chance.

Attend Acquire: Build your Client Base from Contact to Conversion

In this 2 day live event you will:

* Clarify your goals and vision for your company growth

* Get feedback on your sales scripts

* Practice selling to other people in the room

* Leave with sales calls scheduled and pending deals

* Create your 12 month marketing plan

* Identify your ideal client

* Over 30 different client attraction strategies

* Learn the 5 part marketing process to guarantee your campaigns convert

This event is for entrepreneurs, small business owners and team leaders.

Visit the site to learn more: www.amywalkerconsulting.com/acquire

Join the Mastermind

If you are serious about growing your business, one of Amy's Masterminds might be a good fit for you. Amy takes 15 clients per class so that she can work closely with each of you.

In the **Sales and Marketing Mastermind** you will:

Create your sales and marketing strategy

Nail down your messaging, branding, and content creation

Create your social media strategy

Build your sales funnels

Solidify your lead generation and sales

In **The CEO Mastermind** you will:

Build your systems for sales, marketing, and fulfillment

Work on hiring and managing your team

Shift your role from day to day operations and into being the CEO of your business

Stop being the bottle neck to business growth and get serious about company structure

Create a 3 year vision for company growth, and an execution plan

To apply for the mastermind program, email amy@amywalker-consulting.com

COACHING ON DEMAND
THE COACHING YOU NEED AT A PRICE YOU CAN AFFORD

Coaching on Demand

Coaching on Demand brings you the coaching you need at a price you can afford and puts you, the business owner, in the driver's seat.

You decide the areas of business you need to study. You set the pace. You ask the questions. We are here to provide you with customized support that fits your budget.

Coaching on Demand includes

Video business course library

Accountability coaching to ensure you stay on track

Get your questions answered through video chat messaging with your coach

Ability to purchase hours with a business strategist as needed.

For more information visit www.AWCcoachingondemand.com

Made in the USA
Monee, IL
10 October 2023

44361916R10062